HOW OUR WORLD CAME TO BE

BY STANLEY W. ANGRIST

Drawings by Enrico Arno

ALTHOUGH we do not today believe that the world was created by giants or that it burst forth from an egg, in many ways our modern ideas of creation are very much like the stories people told long ago.

This is a book about the creation stories men tell today—stories about binary stars, magnetic fields, and giant star clouds. It clearly explains what scientists now know about the age and nature of the universe and how they came to develop the creation theories most favored by scientists today. The book also discusses, in modern scientific terms, the creation of the solar system—the sun itself, the planets, and our moon.

But this is also a book about the creation myths told by men of ancient times, eons before astronomers began to search the skies with their telescopes. It tells the Indian story of the Lord of the Creatures who came from a golden egg in the sea; and the Crow story about Old Coyote-man who created the world with the help of a pair of diving ducks.

From earliest times, man the scientist, man the poet, man the thinker, and man the observer has spun tales of creation. In How Our World Came to Be, Stanley W. Angrist has written a thought-provoking book about both science and myth that celebrates this very continuity in man's search for knowledge.

HOW OUR WORLD CAME TO BE

HOW OUR WORLD CAME TO BE

CAME TO BE

By Stanley W. Angrist

DRAWINGS BY ENRICO ARNO

THOMAS Y. CROWELL COMPANY · NEW YORK

THANKS ARE DUE to the Mount Wilson and Palomar
Observatories for the photographs on pages 6, 9, 10,
11, 22, 53, and to the National Aeronautics and Space
Administration for the photograph on page 65.

Manufactured in the United States of America

L.C. Card 76–78254

1 2 3 4 5 6 7 8 9 10

TO JOSHUA AND MISHA

CONTENTS

HOW OUR WORLD CAME TO BE

HOW A SCIENTIST LEARNS ABOUT THE WORLD

Long, long ago there was no earth, no sun, no moon.
No stars shone in the heavens.
There was only the darkness of space.

How DID OUR WORLD come into being out of the vast reaches of space? Man has always looked for an answer to this question. Evidence has been found by archaeologists that stories of creation were told by people who lived thousands of years ago. Today, scientists continue the search for explanations of how the earth and the rest of our solar system were formed. But scientists' methods are very different from the methods of the storytellers. Rather than searching in their imaginations for creation stories, as ancient peoples did, today's scientists search in their laboratories with sensitive instruments and study the heavens with giant telescopes for the keys to the mystery of our world's creation.

People of long ago always looked for ways to explain things they saw in nature. But because the men who lived long ago did not have very good ways of studying what they saw, they made up stories to explain the things they observed. As man slowly gathered together the tools and laws of science, his explanations of nature depended less on stories and more on facts and things he could actually see and measure. The early creation stories of man told how the world was born from a golden egg or found by a duck. The creation stories that man tells today are about binary stars, magnetic fields, and giant star clouds. Both the old and the new stories, however, have the same goal—to try to find some answers to a few of nature's riddles. Throughout time man has tried to understand his world and to explain its beginning.

Ancient peoples who lived thousands of miles apart frequently told similar stories of creation. How this could happen in days when there were no telegraphs, no radios, no televisions, and no mailmen to carry letters is a question which no one has been able to answer, and perhaps the answer will never be fully known. Some scholars who have spent their lives studying this subject believe that the minds of men are so much alike the world over that it is not surprising for people who lived thousands of miles from each other to arrive at similar ideas of how the world began. Other students of this subject believe that some of the peoples of long ago traveled great distances by primitive canoe, by horseback, and on foot, carrying their stories of creation with them.

The old stories told by men before they learned to use science to investigate nature are called *myths*. These stories were believable to the men who made them up, but they could not be tested and changed as men learned more facts, and that is the major difference between the myths of long ago and the more recent scientific ideas about creation.

In the past three hundred years man has learned to use the *scientific method* to increase his understanding of the world in which he lives. This method is different from myth-making in a number of important ways. The scientist looks at nature and notes that certain things appear to be true. He calls the evidence he has collected *data* or *observations*. Using these facts he can sometimes work out an explanation for why things happen in a certain way. These explanations are called *theories* or *hypotheses*, but it is well to remember that they represent nothing but educated guesses. By gathering more evidence through more observations the scientist can test his hypothesis again. He must often change it to fit his new observations. This process never stops. Hypotheses are tested, revised, and often discarded as they are replaced by new hypotheses. After a hypothesis has been tested a number of times and is found to fit the observations well, it might then begin to be thought of as a law of nature.

Scientists view their attempts to understand nature much like the construction of a brick house. The hypotheses and theories are the bricks, the scientists the bricklayers. Each brick must be tested and shaped very carefully to make sure it will fit before it is added to the structure. But no theory is ever completely safe, because some scientist might come along at a later time and find a theory that fits the observations better.

With time, this never-completed process of testing and refining hypotheses leads man to a fuller understanding of nature. Unlike myths, which are created in man's imagination and are not changed when new facts are discovered, scientific theories are always subject to change. Newly discovered facts and new interpretations can always cause man's scientific view of the world to be revised.

Just because creation myths were not based on facts does not make them uninteresting. Myths tell about things that were supposed to have happened in primordial time—the time of the beginnings. They are often about how supernatural beings such as giants came to exist and how these super-beings caused the creation of everything else.

People of long ago regarded myths as "true history." The myths explained what people saw and experienced in the world. A myth about the creation of the world was considered true because the existence of the world proved it. A myth about why every person must die sooner or later seemed true because all people do die.

Myths are important because they can tell us what people thought of their world thousands of years before they were able to write about it. Since there were no books, everything that a father or mother had learned could be passed on to children only by word of mouth. The parents told their children the same stories many times. Considering the complexity of some myths, it is surprising how many thousands of years these tales have survived.

One of the most interesting things that you will notice as you read about the modern ideas of creation is that in some ways they are very much like the stories told by the people of long ago. For example, both an ancient story and a modern story suggest that the universe came from an egg, even though the eggs of creation that appear in these stories differ greatly.

Our ideas about creation are continually changing; one replaces another, and it in its turn is discarded for a new one. This has been the history of the development of knowledge ever since that notable day long ago when one of our more adventuresome ancestors finally decided to make a "guess" about how things must have been in the beginning. This process has led to better and better guesses about the origin of the world. Of course, whether man's guesses are right or wrong, the heavens and the earth will continue to turn just the same. But man the scientist and man the poet, man the thinker and man the observer, must continue to spin tales of creation.

A small portion of the Milky Way near the constellation
Sagittarius, toward the center of our galaxy.

A DESCRIPTION OF THE UNIVERSE

IT WOULD BE NICE if one could simply say the world began in the following way and then go ahead and tell how it really did happen. People of long ago did exactly that. Most tribes or groups made up a single story of how they believed the world came to be. These age-old stories contain some very interesting and exciting ideas. Though the stories are colorful, they are not in agreement with the ideas of modern science.

Man today does not believe that the world was created by giants or that it burst forth from an egg. But scientists studying creation, like scientists in other areas, are constantly testing, refining, and discarding ideas on the subject. For that reason there have been a number of different creation ideas suggested in modern times; and frequently theories put forth by different scientists are in conflict with one another. Before these theories are explored it will be necessary to consider briefly the makeup of our universe, galaxy, and solar system.

What Is in the Universe

Stars, of which our sun is just one of billions in the universe, are among the most important kinds of heavenly bodies. They are gigantic nuclear furnaces that turn the lightest of all gases, hydrogen, into another very light gas, helium. This conversion of hydrogen to helium takes place by way of the fusion process that is used in the hydrogen bomb. The changing of hydrogen into helium in the sun, the star nearest to the earth, releases the tremendous amount of light and heat that make life on earth possible.

To help them map the sky, people of long ago grouped stars into imaginary pictures in the heavens. Star groups that have been given names are called *constellations*. Ursa Major, Cassiopeia, and Orion are three constellations that are usually visible in the skies over the United States.

If you look at the sky on a dark, clear night you will see a very faint, whitish band of light that stretches across the sky. For thousands of years this band has been called *the Milky Way*. Astronomers sometimes refer to it, plus all the stars that can be seen with the naked eye and millions of other nearby stars, as "the Galaxy." It is now known that the Milky Way consists of countless numbers of stars too close together to be seen as separate stars without using a telescope and that our sun and earth are part of it. The word *galaxy* is used to define a very large collection of stars and other heavenly bodies, more or less isolated in space. Galaxies are sometimes called island universes.

Our galaxy is rotating like a great wheel, and the millions of stars move around its center somewhat as the earth and the other planets rotate around our sun. If it were possible to view our galaxy from another planet an enormous distance away, it would look something like the galaxy shown in the photograph on the opposite page, located in the constellation Ursa Major, of which the Big Dipper is a part. Astronomers used

A spiral galaxy in the Ursa Major constellation. The arms, made up of dust and millions of stars, coil out from the center like the vanes of a pinwheel.

A portion of the giant gaseous clouds that form the Great Nebula in the "sword" of Orion.

to think that the universe stopped with our galaxy. They now know that the Milky Way is just one of the hundreds of millions of galaxies that populate the universe.

The Milky Way and countless other star systems in space have the shape of flattened disks with spiral arms coiling out from their centers. These spiral arms contain, in addition to millions of stars, giant clouds of dust and gas. These clouds are called *nebulae*. Of the nebulae near the earth, the brightest is the Great Nebula in the "sword" of the constellation Orion. All nebulae consist mostly of hydrogen gas, and many of

10

them glow faintly either because stars are being created in them or because they reflect the light of nearby bright stars.

Astronomers have many special tools to assist them in their study of the universe. One of the most important of their tools is the telescope. Most reflecting telescopes consist of two main parts: a curved mirror to gather the light from the object being viewed, and a lens system to magnify the image formed by the mirror. Today, an important addition to any telescope used for serious study is a camera that can photograph anything the astronomer observes with the telescope.

The 200-inch Hale telescope at the Palomar Observatory in California. The telescope is pointing directly overhead. The observer sits in the little tube near the top of the telescope. The 200-inch mirror, which cannot be seen in this photograph, is directly beneath him at the bottom of the cagelike structure.

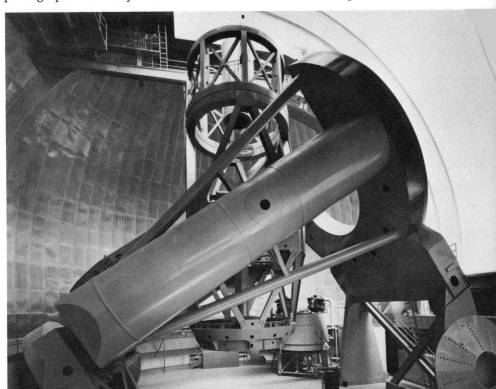

In the last thirty years astronomers have turned to a new instrument to help them learn about the objects in the heavens. Almost all galaxies and nebulae send out another kind of energy besides light. They send out radio waves. Radio astronomers have built huge antennas to catch these signals and focus them in a way similar to that in which the mirror collects and focuses light in an ordinary telescope. To gain a better understanding of the universe, scientists have added the information obtained by studying the radio waves from distant objects in the universe to that obtained from the photographs made by ordinary telescopes.

Many astronomers have directed their telescopes much closer to home than the nebulae of our Milky Way. They study the star that is most important to us, the sun, and its satellites, the planets. The sun, its planets, and the comets that cross the heavens from time to time are commonly lumped together and called by one name—the *solar system.*

The *planets* are bodies that travel around the sun and give out no light of their own. They can be seen only when sunlight is reflected from their surfaces. Besides the earth there are eight major planets in our solar system. The nine planets have a total of thirty-one moons, but without a telescope we can see only the one moon that orbits the earth.

Asteroids, or minor planets, are among the smallest members of our solar system. They are small stony or metallic objects that range in size from a few miles to several hundred miles across. Like the nine planets, they travel in orbits about the sun. Most asteroids are located between the orbits of Mars and Jupiter.

Meteors are also considered a part of our solar system. They are small stonelike bodies that enter the earth's atmosphere. As they do so, they get so hot from the friction of the air that they generally burn up before they land, producing a brilliant flash of light as they fall.

Most *comets*, once believed to be from outside our solar system, are now thought to be part of it. Like the planets and the asteroids, they too seem to move in definite orbits around the sun. They appear to be somewhat related to meteors and perhaps to asteroids. The head of a comet is a collection of small meteorlike fragments. Comets' trails consist of very fine gases and dust thrown out from the head. Comets shine partly by reflected light and partly because sunlight causes their gases to glow.

The Size of the Solar System

The solar system is by one measure a tiny, insignificant speck and by another measure almost too big for most people to understand. As a part of the universe it is almost too small to be noticed—a rowboat in an endless ocean. But by any ordinary measure the solar system is huge. It is much, much bigger than anything most people usually think about. Imagine that the sun is a ball 6 inches across. (It really is 864,000 miles across.) The earth, in comparison with the 6-inch sun, would be a dot about 1/16 inch across, which is a little thicker than the lead in an ordinary pencil. In the imaginary scale-model system the tiny earth would be 54 feet from the 6-inch ball. The nearest star to the 1/16-inch dot (earth) would be 2,000 miles in the model system.

Comparisons made with even the imaginary 6-inch sun lead to numbers that are far too large for describing galaxies.

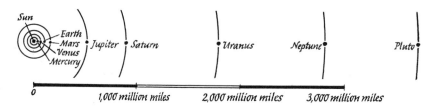

The average distances of the planets from the sun. Pluto is more than 100 times farther from the sun than Mercury.

Astronomers use another kind of measure, called the *light-year*, to describe great distances.

Light travels very fast. It takes only a little more than a second for light to go from the moon to the earth. The distance from the earth to the moon could be called a *light-second*. It takes about eight minutes for light to travel to us from the sun, and thus one could say the distance between the earth and the sun is eight *light-minutes*. But even the light-minute is too small a yardstick to use in describing distance in our galaxy and the universe. For these giant distances it is most convenient to use the *light-year*—the distance light travels in a year. One light-year equals 5,870,000,000,000 miles. That number can be read as 5,870 billion miles. It takes light a little over four *years* to reach us from the *nearest* star.

Our galaxy, the Milky Way, is a collection of stars that is shaped somewhat like a dinner plate. It is more than 100,000 light-years across, with our sun located about 30,000 light-years away from the center in one of the thinner sections of the dinner plate.

Using the giant light-year as a yardstick only helps a little in understanding how immense our galaxy really is. And yet

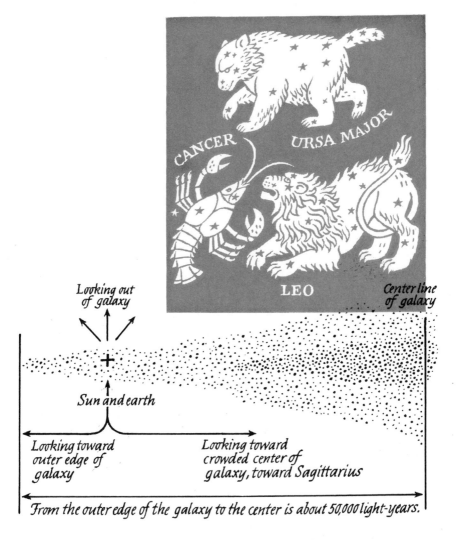

The location of the sun and its planets in our galaxy. Our sun is about 30,000 light-years from the center of the galaxy.

when it is considered that our galaxy is just one galaxy out of billions in the universe, it is possible to begin to appreciate how tiny even the Milky Way is.

15

The Age of the Solar System

In addition to having measured the size of our galaxy and our solar system fairly accurately, scientists have also been able to determine the approximate ages of the earth and the rest of the solar system. They use a method called radioactive dating, which requires an understanding of atoms.

All ordinary matter is composed of atoms. Atoms are tiny bits of matter, far too small to be seen even with microscopes. Each atom consists of smaller particles called *neutrons, protons,* and *electrons.* Not all atoms are the same size; some are big and some are small. The size of an atom is mainly determined by the number of protons and neutrons that make up its nucleus and the number of electrons that form the electron cloud around the nucleus. The number of protons in the nucleus determines what kind of atom it is—for example, whether it is an atom of iron, an atom of copper, or an atom of oxygen. Any substance whose atoms all have the same number of protons in the nucleus is called an *element.* Elements cannot be separated into simpler substances by ordinary chemical methods.

A proton is the positively charged particle found in the nucleus of an atom. A neutron is a second type of tiny particle found in the nucleus of the atom. It carries no electric charge. The electron is the minuscule, negatively charged particle that creates the cloud around the nucleus. The charge on a particle tells how the particle would behave if, for example, it were possible to bring it near a positive terminal on a battery. A proton, carrying a positive charge, would be pushed away from a positive terminal, since like charges repel each other. An electron, carrying a negative charge, would be attracted to the positive terminal, since opposite charges attract each other. A neutron, carrying no charge, would be neither attracted nor repelled.

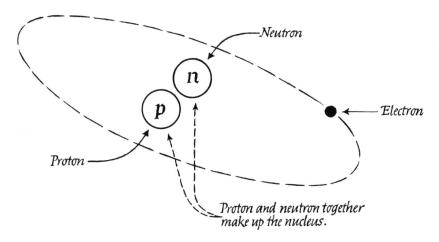

The parts of an atom. The atom illustrated here is deuterium, sometimes called heavy hydrogen because it has twice the mass of ordinary hydrogen; it occurs rarely in nature.

In all atoms there is a force, or pull, that holds all the protons and neutrons together in the nucleus. It is called the *binding force* and it is usually stronger than the electric force of repulsion that exists between the like charges of the protons in the nucleus. But in certain large atoms that contain many protons and neutrons, the electric forces are very strong, and the binding force is not great enough to stop the atom from throwing out a proton or an electron. Such atoms are said to be unstable. When an unstable atom ejects a proton or an electron, the remaining protons, neutrons, and electrons constitute a new atom. These unstable atoms combine to make up *radioactive elements*, such as uranium and radium.

70357

The fact that radioactive elements continue to eject particles until they become the stable elements helium and lead was discovered early in this century. Scientists also discovered how long it takes a piece of uranium to change completely into lead and helium; in 1913 this information was used to fix the age of some rocks at about one billion years.

Using radioactivity to date objects is really very simple. Each year a small part of radioactive uranium is changed into lead and helium by the ejection of particles. This means that, as the years pass, the amount of lead in any piece of uranium will slowly increase. Thus, a scientist simply takes a sample of rock and measures the amount of uranium and the amount of lead it contains. Since the scientist knows how many years it takes for a certain amount of uranium to change into lead, he can now compute from his lead and uranium measurements how old the rock sample is. From this information he can estimate the age of the earth's crust. This method of dating rocks is not perfect, but it is believed to give answers that are fairly reliable. Various radioactive materials have been used as atomic clocks to estimate the age of rock on earth and of meteorites from our solar system. These measurements indicate that the earth and the solar system came into being about four and one-half billion years ago.

THE EGG STORY OF CREATION

 THE NOTION that the universe might
have come into being from a giant
egg is not a new idea. Some egg
stories of creation are thousands of
years old and they have been told
by various peoples in every part of
the world. Perhaps early man's observations of the hatching of a
chick gave him the idea that the very universe itself began in
this way. From an apparently lifeless form—the egg—life began. Here was a creation process that was both understand-
able and familiar.

One of the many egg stories comes from the people who
practice the Hindu religion in India. They say that in the beginning there were only hot, swirling waters in complete
darkness. Except for the waters no thing had shape or form
until out of the blackness a golden egg mysteriously appeared
in the rolling sea. After a long time the egg finally hatched
and the Lord of Creatures revealed himself. He had been
growing in the egg for a very long time. He was able to split
the egg, so the story goes, by thinking about it. The upper
half of the shell became the heavens, while the bottom half
became the earth and all the things on it. Between the two, the
air and the clouds formed, with the ground floating on the
waters.

Out of this egg came the ancestor of every person and every thing, with a thousand feet, a thousand arms, a thousand eyes, and a thousand heads. He was, according to the Hindus, every thing, every animal, every plant, and every man—in short, all that has been, all that is, and all that will be.

The Chinese tell a different egg myth, which is at least fifteen hundred years old. Before either heaven or earth came to be, the unformed universe was said to look like a hen's egg. Inside this egg was born a giant named P'an-Ku. After eighteen thousand years the egg cracked open. The heavy, coarse parts in the egg, the yolk, formed the earth; the light pure parts, the egg white, made up the sky. Every day the sky rose by ten feet and every day the earth grew deeper by ten feet, so that after another eighteen thousand years had passed, P'an-Ku's body was as tall as the distance between heaven and earth. Other legends about P'an-Ku tell how, after his death, parts of his body became mountains, his tears became rivers, his breath became the wind, his voice thunder, and his eyes lightning.

These ancient myths about giants that sprang from eggs are not so very different, in a general way, from a group of theories of creation told today. These theories might be called evolutionary creation hypotheses. They state that the universe has changed greatly from what it was like in the beginning. These theories argue that in the billions of years that have passed, the universe has slowly evolved or changed into its present form, just as P'an-Ku himself slowly changed. Furthermore, they predict that over a very long period of time, the universe will continue to change.

The Giant Atom

Georges Lemaître, a Belgian physicist who was also a Roman Catholic priest, presented an evolutionary theory of the creation of the universe that is both interesting and puzzling. Calculations that he made led him to believe that sometime in the ancient past the universe was packed into a single, giant atom. He called it the "primeval atom" because he supposed it contained nothing but protons and electrons. Lemaître believed that this enormous atom, or "super egg" as some have called it, exploded, breaking up into smaller and smaller collections of radioactive atoms called atom stars. The explosions and disintegrations continued until everything was reduced to the fundamental building blocks of matter: protons and electrons. (It is not surprising that Lemaître ignored neutrons in his theory; they were not discovered until after he suggested his primitive atom idea.) Lemaître then reasoned that after the giant atom had reduced itself completely to electrons and protons, these tiny chunks of matter regrouped themselves into the various atoms found in the universe today. Lemaître said that these happenings must have been similar to a giant fireworks display.

It would be hard to imagine an explosion as gigantic as the one that Lemaître hypothesized, but spectacular though smaller explosions do occasionally occur in the heavens. In the year 1054, Chinese astronomers saw a star explode in the Taurus constellation. The remains are now called the Crab Nebula and it is still expanding at a speed of about 70 million miles a day. Stars that explode and become extremely bright for a short while are called *supernova*.

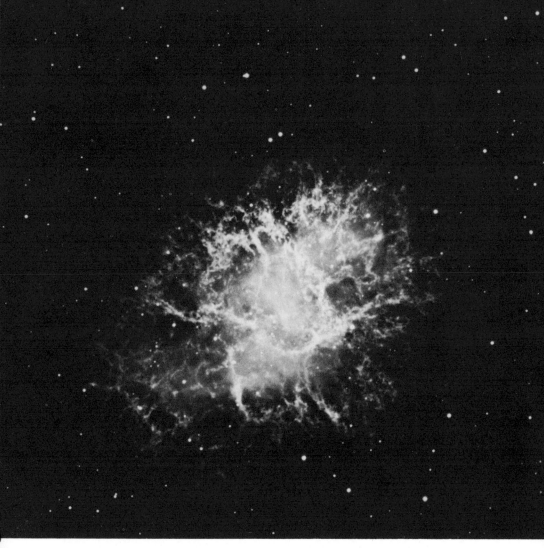

The remains of a supernova that exploded in the year 1054. Now called the Crab Nebula, it is found in the constellation Taurus.

Shortly after Lemaître started to work on his theory, Edwin Hubble, an American astronomer, announced that his astronomical observations showed that all distant galaxies were moving away from us. In fact, he noted that everything in the universe is in motion with respect to everything else. Our earth rotates around the sun, our solar system moves toward the star Vega, and the Milky Way Galaxy rotates slowly about a center that is 26,000 light-years away from the earth, beyond the star constellation Sagittarius. Some astronomers suggested that perhaps it was the explosions of the primeval atom that put the parts of the universe into flight in all directions.

Lemaître's creation hypothesis supposed that nothing existed outside of the giant atom. The universe, including space itself, was completely enclosed in the atom. Furthermore, time began when the giant atom exploded. It is difficult to understand what Lemaître meant when he said there was no time before the explosion and no space outside of the atom.

Lemaître's theory was an important step in the direction of trying to learn how our universe came to be. But it left several questions unanswered. One important problem that troubled scientists was that the theory did not explain how the heavier atoms—those that contained large numbers of protons—were put together from the small atoms, which resulted from the breaking up of the original giant atom. It is not surprising that Lemaître's theory did not explain these events, since it was first published completely in 1931. It was only after this date that a large part of our knowledge about the inside of atoms was gained.

Even though it failed to explain the atom-building process satisfactorily, the Lemaître theory is still considered important historically. It was the first theory to contain some explanation of the universal expansion as observed by Hubble.

Atom Building in the Beginning

The idea that the universe evolved from some simpler and more compact state is still considered an acceptable creation theory by many astronomers. George Gamow, a Russian-American physicist with an unusually fine sense of humor and a rare gift for explaining scientific ideas to nonscientists, studied Lemaître's theory and was able to remove some of its weaknesses. Gamow was convinced that the universe had evolved over billions of years, chiefly because he was struck by the "strange coincidence" that many of the methods used to guess the age of the universe all point to the same age range of more than 5 billion and less than 15 billion years. He reasoned that if the entire universe did not begin at the same time, astronomers would find some evidence that different parts of the universe have greatly different ages. Astronomers have not found such evidence.

The universe's age has been estimated by a number of different methods. Perhaps the most important method is the one that relates the brightness and temperature of a star to its age. Studies have shown that stars that are initially small are cooler and live longer than those that start out as bright, massive stars. It is also possible to compute how long it takes for atoms of hydrogen to turn into atoms of helium in a star. This atomic conversion is called the *fusion* process and is the same one that causes the tremendous release of energy in the hydrogen bomb. Using information about a star's brightness, temperature, size, and rate of hydrogen conversion enables astronomers to estimate a star's age. (Our sun has been estimated to have an age of about 6 billion years and will probably go dark in 10 to 15 billion years.) If one finds a very old star by this method, then it can be supposed that its age is very close to the age of the universe. Thus the old star acts somewhat as a clock for the universe.

Another way of estimating the universe's age is by making use of the fact that the universe appears to be expanding in all directions. This method can be simply explained as follows: Imagine looking out the front window of your house and seeing a car driving away from you up the street. If you know how far away the car is, and how fast it is going, you can figure out how long ago the car passed in front of your house. Dividing the distance by the speed gives the time.

If Lemaître's, Hubble's, or Gamow's evolutionary theories are true, the time since the beginning of the expansion represents the age of the universe. Astronomers' measurements lead them to believe that the speed of distant galaxies is increasing at the rate of about 14 miles a second for every million light-years that they are away from us. This number, called Hubble's constant, after the same Edwin Hubble who first observed the expansion of the universe, can be used in a simple calculation to arrive at an age for the universe of 10 to 13 billion years. In fact, most of the ten or so methods used to estimate the age of the universe lead to a number fairly close to this.

Although the universe might have started its great expansion 10 to 13 billion years ago, astronomers do not believe that our sun and solar system came into being at that time. It took at least several billion years for our sun to shrink into a mass of gas able to sustain a nuclear reaction capable of producing heat and light.

The fact that so many methods point to the same age for the universe encouraged Gamow to try to improve the Lemaître theory of creation. Gamow reasoned that any creation theory would have to be built around two important observations that scientists had made about the universe: (1) that everything in the universe appears to have been created at about the same time; and (2) that the entire universe is expanding—the galaxies seem to be in flight from each other.

Gamow believed that about 10 to 13 billion years ago the entire universe consisted of a tremendous amount of heavy gas of neutrons; it was the primeval egg again. These neutrons—the uncharged particles found in the nucleus of atoms—were packed so close together that they were very hot and under great pressure. So far, this theory sounds much like the Lemaître theory, but Gamow added that this collection of neutrons was so large that it must be called infinite in size. Then Gamow suggested that instead of one initial explosion occurring, as in the case of the Lemaître atom, an infinite number of smaller explosions took place to start the universal expansion.

Now Gamow had to devise an explanation for how the different kinds of atoms that make up the elements were formed from the neutrons in the giant egg. An atom consists of a nucleus packed with positively charged protons plus one or more neutrons and with one or more electrons in orbit around the central nucleus. The problem of forming the different atoms that make up the elements is one of combining various numbers of neutrons and protons into nuclei. Then a number of electrons equal to the number of protons in the nucleus have to be supplied to swarm in a cloud about the nucleus.

According to Gamow's theory, as soon as the explosions began, the universe started to expand very rapidly. A neutron

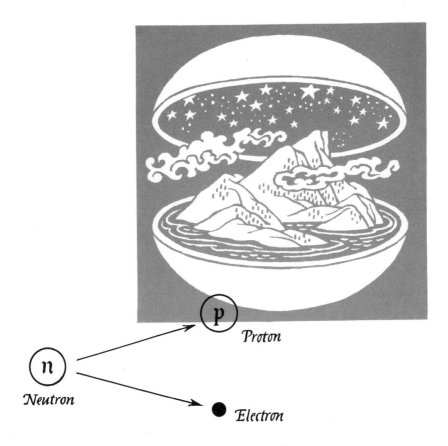

The decay of a neutron into a proton and an electron.

does not remain a neutron for very long if it is outside an atom. That is, in about 13 minutes or so it decays or changes into a proton and an electron. In the first minutes following the explosions, neutrons, protons, and electrons were so hot and were flying around with such high speed, they could not stick together to start making atoms. Gamow called this mixture of particles *ylem*—the name that Aristotle gave to primordial matter. As the universe kept on expanding and the temperature of ylem dropped, protons and neutrons began to stick together forming *deuterons*, the nucleus of a heavy form of hydrogen, and heavier elements. The element-building process is believed by Gamow to have continued for about 30 minutes.

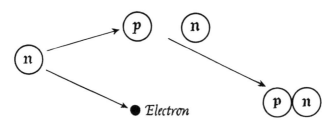

Some neutrons decayed into protons and electrons with the protons combining with other free neutrons to form deuterons.

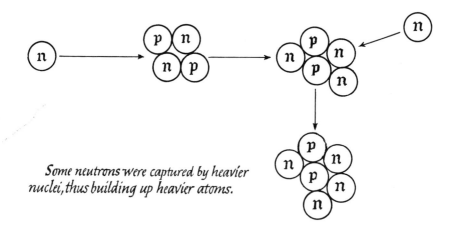

Some neutrons were captured by heavier nuclei, thus building up heavier atoms.

Some of the atom-building processes that Gamow believed took place in the first half hour after the primeval atom exploded.

A Push-Me, Pull-You Theory

A theory that suggests that our universe started from an extremely compressed concentration of matter and energy naturally raises the question: How did it get into that state in the first place, and what made it expand? One possible answer to this question has been given by Ernest J. Öpik, an astronomer at the Armagh Observatory in Northern Ireland, who has suggested that two fundamental forces exist throughout the universe: One is the force that tries to push matter apart, which began with the explosions of the giant atom; the second is the pulling-together force of gravity, which causes material to collect and form things like planets. (It is also the force that pulls a pebble tossed into the air back to earth.) Öpik believes that the universe will keep on growing until the pushing-apart force is overcome by the attractive, or inward-pulling, force. Then the universe will begin to fall in upon itself until another single giant atom is formed again. At that point the pushing-apart force will be stronger than the inward-pulling force and the giant atom will start to expand again. His calculations led him to believe that the universe may be expanding and collapsing once every 30 billion years. These ideas when added to the Gamow theory offer a possible description of the universe before, during, and after the present grand expansion.

Evolutionary Theories of Creation

The Gamow theory raises many questions as it attempts to answer the riddle of creation. However, it does agree with many of the facts modern science knows about the universe. It also agrees with what scientists know about the age of the universe. It can explain in a satisfactory way the observed universal expansion. And it does predict fairly well the observed abundance of the elements found in nature. For these reasons the Gamow theory represents the most complete and convincing evolutionary hypothesis of creation presented so far.

The evolutionary method of creation as proposed by Lemaître, Gamow, and others is at once both interesting and puzzling. The questions these theories raise must have been similar to questions raised by thoughtful Indians or Chinese a thousand years ago when they tried to think about what the universe was like before the Lord of Creatures revealed himself or before P'an-Ku broke his egg.

In fact, there is much evidence that our scientific ideas about creation are not new. Even the notion that the universe is alternately expanding and contracting is not very original. There is a Hindu belief, probably thousands of years old, that Brahma, the creator, calmly sits forever exhaling and inhaling the universe through his nostrils.

A SOMETHING-OUT-OF-NOTHING IDEA

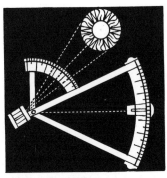

OTHER ASTRONOMERS do not agree that the universe is exploding out of a "super egg." They present a completely different idea: the theory that the universe *had no beginning*. They say that the creation process is continuous and never ending; the universe has always and will always consist of billions of very hot stars floating in an infinitely vast sea of cold, dark space. In some respects this idea is similar to the creation myth told by the peoples who lived long ago in southern Sweden and Norway, the islands in the Baltic Sea, and the plains in northern Germany.

There was nothing, according to these people, but an enormous crack that stretched from the icy darkness and mist in the north, called Niflheim, to the regions of fire in the south, known as Muspelsheim. Out of the fire, ice, darkness, and mist the land and the sea were formed. Rivers came from the south and flowed to the land of ice—there they soon froze and disappeared in the icy vastness. Slowly, these frozen river waters filled the giant crack, and then the warm south winds began to melt the ice. This was the beginning of the first spring.

The first little trickle of water on the surface of the ice-filled world was the ancestor of every living thing, because the drops of water were given energy by the warm air from the south and gathered to make a living body, that of the first giant, Ymir. He was, according to this legend, the founder of all the giants and of the other gods these people worshiped.

Soon Ymir was joined by a giant cow called Audhumla, who also arose from the melted ice. For this reason the cow was considered sacred among all the animals. Four rivers of milk flowed from Audhumla's udders as she licked the ice and nourished herself on the salt it contained. While the giant Ymir drank her milk and gathered strength, the cow managed to bring forth another living creature from the warm drops that her tongue sent trickling down the ice; he was called Buri and was to be the forefather of the gods.

Eventually, the grandsons of Buri killed Ymir and used the parts of his body to make the various parts of the world. His flesh became the earth, his bones became mountains, and his skull became the dome of the heavens. His brain created the clouds that spread across the sky.

Once the gods had made Ymir's skull the shell of the heavens, it caught the millions of sparks that had been racing out of the sun and disappearing into the icy wilderness. These sparks, according to this story, became the stars that twinkle in the night sky. And thus the whole universe came from the nothingness of a cold, dark, giant crevasse.

Perhaps it is not surprising to encounter a myth in which something is created from nothing, but some scientists hesitate to accept a scientific theory with that as a basis. This idea, suggested by three British astronomers, Hermann Bondi, Thomas Gold, and Fred Hoyle, holds that the universe is continuously being created—from nothing.

Edwin Hubble found, as has already been noted, that all

the galaxies appear to be moving away from each other. He also found that the farther away a galaxy is from us, the faster it is moving. This fact is called Hubble's law. This law sets a limit on how much of the universe can be seen from the earth. If a galaxy is moving away from us at the same speed at which light travels (186,000 miles per second), then a light beam from that galaxy can never reach the earth. The distance at which this happens has been calculated and is found to be about 13 billion light-years. This is called the limit of the *observable universe,* and most scientists believe that nothing can ever be known about objects beyond this distance.

Since the galaxies are moving away from us, one might suppose, then, that in a few billion years the observable universe will contain our galaxy and one or two other nearby galaxies. The continuous-creation theory says that this is not so; because matter is being continuously created the supply of galaxies will never be exhausted.

The Creation of Hydrogen

Where does the matter come from to create new galaxies? The hypothesis of Bondi, Gold, and Hoyle simply says that matter is being made out of nothing all the time! They claim that hydrogen is being created: At one instant the atoms do not exist, an instant later they do. They believe that it is hydrogen because it is both the most abundant element in the universe and the simplest of all the atoms, consisting of one proton and one electron. This idea of creating something from nothing may seem like a very strange idea, but it is probably no more strange than the notion that our universe sprang forth from a single giant atom.

The continuous-creation theory states that matter is being created all the time just fast enough to replace the matter that disappears over the edge of that part of the universe that is knowable to us. The rate at which matter is being created and lost over the edge of the observable universe has been calculated. According to this theory, not more than one atom is created per year in the space occupied by a skyscraper. Because the universe is so large, even this quantity of creation amounts to billions and billions of tons of hydrogen every second. The creation-of-matter theory, according to the scientists who have proposed it, answers the question, What force is driving the galaxies apart? They believe that the new material continuously being made produces a pressure that causes the universe to grow.

Bondi, Gold, and Hoyle believe that after the hydrogen is formed, it gathers in great clouds. The giant clouds break into smaller clouds, which shrink further, grow hot, and become stars. The stars spin and perhaps give birth to some planets like ours. The hydrogen atoms in the center of these stars cook in nuclear reactions to produce helium (just as our sun does) and eventually form all the other elements.

The new stars and galaxies pass through the various stages of life and ultimately fade away, to be replaced by new ones. For stars the fading out is actually their death process, caused by the burning up of all their hydrogen fuel. According to this theory, as galaxies die, two things are happening at the same time. The stars in the galaxies are gradually growing old and fading away, and they are also passing completely out of the observable universe, never to return. Thus, the rebirth and death of the universe never ends and goes on forever and ever.

If the Universe Were a Lake

James Coleman, an American physicist, suggested an easy way to think about this creation story. Imagine a large lake with a dam at one end in which many different kinds of fish are swimming. The lake in this case is the observable universe, and the water in the lake plays the role of space. The different types of fish represent the galaxies, stars, and nebulae. The lake receives additional water from rain, which causes some of the water and some of the fish, both live ones and dead ones, to flow over the dam.

The fish cannot see beyond the edges of the lake, which represent the limits of their universe; however, they do know by observation that part of their universe is continually disappearing (by going over the dam) and that more universe always appears to take its place by some unknown process (rain). Now a really clever school of fish (perhaps astronomers like Bondi, Gold, and Hoyle) could figure out a theory to explain how their universe works.

The water level in the lake remains at the same height because that part of the fish's universe that is constantly disappearing is at the same time being replaced by an equal amount of rain water. Even though the water level stays the same, many things are going on in the lake. Various kinds of fish are born at different times, grow up, and die. These fish, alive or lifeless, may be swept over the dam at the end of the lake. This is analogous to the birth, life, and death of galaxies and stars that is seen going on in our universe all the time.

This theory is different in some ways from all the other ideas of nature. Galaxies, stars, planets, and men are born, grow old, and die—but the universe remains. It was here in

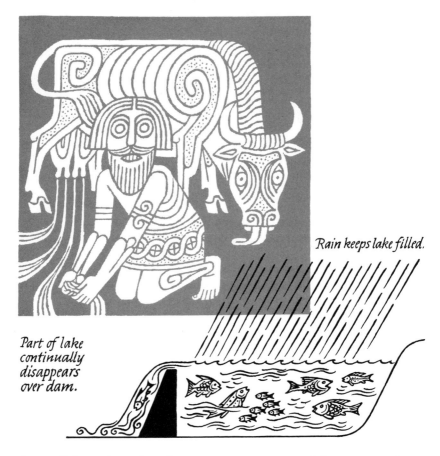

Rain keeps lake filled.

Part of lake continually disappears over dam.

James Coleman's analogy for continuous creation of the universe. Some fish (stars) continually leave the observable universe by passing over the dam. Like individual stars, individual fish go through a life cycle and are replaced by others.

the past, it is here now, and it will always be here in the future.

Giant Egg or Something from Nothing?

Which of these two theories is correct? Did the universe start with a big bang about 10 billion years ago or has it always been here, constantly being renewed by fresh hydrogen made out of nothing? The answer to this question is not known. Some scientists believe that neither theory is wholly correct; that other explanations could be constructed that use parts of each of these theories. Others believe that a new theory unrelated to either of these two is required. Supporters of each of these creation ideas can produce evidence to support their theories.

The evolutionary, or big-bang, supporters point to all the evidence that says something big happened in the universe about 10 billion years ago. They can also make measurements using radioactive materials that show that the earth, the moon, and the planets all came into being about 5 billion years ago. However, their critics note that all these estimates of age come from bodies in our galaxy and our galaxy is only one of billions of galaxies in the universe. The critics ask, Is it reasonable to believe that all the galaxies came into being 10 billion years ago just because ours did?

A different argument in favor of the big-bang, or evolutionary, theory compares the development of the universe with development of organisms in the biological world. It is accepted by almost everyone that all the present animal life on earth, including man, results from a long series of biological changes during which all animal forms evolved from very simple creatures or organisms into the very complicated ones of today. Big-bang theory supporters believe that evolution is the fundamental law which controls the complete physical universe as a whole and that biological evolution is just one example of the operation of this law. If this is so, our complicated universe would be the result of an evolutionary process from a system that was originally very simple. In the same way, man is believed to have evolved from simpler organisms.

On the other hand, one of the most convincing pieces of evidence in favor of the continuous-creation theory is the large amount of free hydrogen atoms found throughout the universe. Not only do hydrogen atoms in the free state populate the space between the stars, but hydrogen is the main fuel of the stars. Scientists have estimated that more than three quarters of all the matter in the universe is pure hydrogen. Those scientists who argue in favor of the continuous-creation theory claim that hydrogen is abundant because it is being made all the time throughout the universe.

There is also evidence against the continuous-creation theory. According to astronomers Bondi, Gold, and Hoyle, the universe should be the same everywhere. That is, there ought to be about the same number of galaxies in every part of the universe since hydrogen is being created everywhere at about the same rate. Using a radio telescope to detect the presence of far-distant galaxies, Martin Ryle of England's Cambridge University has found that at great distances from the earth the galaxies are not evenly spaced as the continuous-creation theory says they should be. Ryle therefore believes that this theory cannot be correct. His results must have additional confirmation from other scientists before his conclusion can be widely accepted, however. Bondi, Gold, Hoyle, and other scientists as well, disagree with Ryle on the value and meaning of his results. So again one finds scientists stacking up evidence for one theory and other scientists knocking it down. Will the origin of the universe in which we live ever be known? There is no way to answer that question today.

THE CREATION OF OUR
SOLAR SYSTEM

IN ONE WAY OR ANOTHER our universe came to be. It is not necessary for us to know exactly how it came to be in order to try to answer the smaller question, How was our solar system, the sun and its planets, born out of that universe?

In trying to answer this question many astronomers looked for a special event that could have caused the creation of the planets. Scientists in the past often assumed that the planets were created when, a long time ago, another star—a visitor or intruder—passed very close to our sun.

The Tidal Theory

People of long ago frequently looked in places of which they were fearful for explanations of how their world came to be. Because they knew little about lakes or oceans, they supposed that they contained the answers to many things they did not understand, and they made up myths based on their guesses and their fears. An example of this type of creation myth is the one told by the Crow Indians.

They believed that in the beginning there was water everywhere and no ground could be seen anywhere. The hero of the Crow Indian story of creation is called Old Coyote-man. He was thought to have both the cunning of the coyote and the energy of the sun. This combination allowed him to bring everything into being from the endless waters in which he floated. He was troubled by this lack of land and he wondered where he would find a world. After Old Coyote-man drifted first this way then that way for a long time, two ducks spotted him and swam toward him as there was no other thing of interest to look at—everywhere else there was only water. Old Coyote-man told the ducks he was looking for the world and asked them to help him in his search. The ducks agreed that it would be good to find the world and they asked how they could help.

Coyote told one duck to dive down in the water and look for the land. After the third dive the duck did not come back to the surface. Old Coyote-man was discouraged, but he thought he would try one more thing. He asked the other duck to dive down and try to bring back some mud on his beak. The remaining duck, after four tries, finally came up with some mud. The Coyote-man took that mud and scattered it about him and it became the earth. He molded and shaped rivers, bays, mountains, and valleys in the mud. After he had shaped the earth he used the mud to make buffaloes, horses, other animals, and men and women. Thus the earth was formed.

There is a scientific theory that also proposes that our world was born out of an ocean—an ocean of hot gases. It was suggested early in the twentieth century by a famous British scientist, Sir James Jeans. Jeans thought that the planets were created when a star passed near the sun and raised a tide on it. Anyone who has spent time at the ocean side has seen tides rise and fall. The waters rise because they are being pulled up by the moon. Indeed, every object in the universe exerts a pull on every other object in the universe.

This fact was first stated as a law of nature by Sir Isaac Newton. Newton was born on Christmas Day, 1642, in a small village in England. His contributions to science were so numerous and important that he is now looked upon as one of the world's greatest scientific geniuses. Jeans's theory about the creation of the solar system is based on Newton's laws.

Newton in his First Law of Motion said that any object at rest would remain at rest, and any moving object would continue to move in a *straight line,* unless acted on by a force—a push or a pull. The fact that the moon revolves around the earth and that the planets revolve around the sun told Newton that some force must be acting on these bodies to cause them to move along *ellipse,* or egg-shaped, paths instead of moving in straight lines. He concluded that the moon must be revolving around the earth because it is attracted to it. He also noted that objects on the earth's surface fall down because they are attracted to the earth. Then he wondered if these two attraction forces—the one that makes the moon revolve around the earth and the one that makes the apple fall to the ground under the tree—might not be the same force. To support his reasoning, Newton had to determine whether the earth's pull on a body changes as the body is moved farther and farther away from the earth. Newton examined closely the work of another scientist, Johannes Kepler. From his study of Kepler's work, Newton concluded that the force that pulls the apple toward the earth, making it fall, and the force that pulls the moon toward the earth, making it circle the earth, were indeed the same force. From this work Newton was able to arrive at his now famous Law of Gravitation. This law states that everything in the universe, large or small, exerts a pull on everything else. These attraction forces between bodies are sometimes called *gravity* forces.

Newton found that the amount of pull between two bodies depends on two things: their mass and the distance between them. The *mass* of a body is measured by the amount of force that must be applied to it to bring it up to a desired speed in a given amount of time; the larger a body's mass, the larger the push it must be given.

The greater the masses of two bodies, the greater will be the attractive force between them. Two small marbles sitting a few inches from each other on a desk top attract each other, but because the mass of the marbles is small, the force between them is very small compared to the force exerted on them by the giant earth.

The greater the distance between two bodies, the smaller is the attractive force between them. At a height of only 1,800 miles above the surface of the earth, the earth's pull on any object is only one half of what it would be on the surface.

Tides are another demonstration of Newton's Law of Gravitation. The moon exerts a pull on the earth and the earth exerts an equal pull on the moon, but the pull is not great enough to move them closer together. The moon pulls on both the solid earth itself and on the earth's ocean waters. Because the earth is solid it is pulled as one piece, while the earth's ocean waters bulge when the moon pulls on them. This bulge in the ocean waters is the tide. The tidal bulge in the ocean tends to follow the moon as it orbits the earth.

In his theory Sir James Jeans suggested that our planetary system was formed when a passing star came close to the sun.

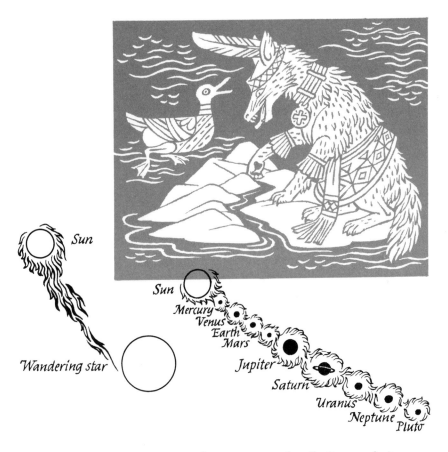

According to Sir James Jeans, the gravitational pull of a wandering star removed some of the sun's mass. This mass stayed in the neighborhood of the sun and upon cooling, formed into the planets.

This passing star was thought by Jeans to have raised giant tides on the sun, causing its shape to be greatly changed. Jeans believed that some matter was pulled away from the sun and it followed the path of the passing star and formed a long trail of gas. As the intruder star moved farther and farther away from the sun, its gravitational pull on the gaseous matter became weaker as compared with the sun's gravitational pull on it. Finally the sun's pull won control and the long trail of gas swung into orbit about the sun.

According to Jeans, this gaseous trail could not remain stringlike for very long. Any object that is long enough and thin enough can be easily broken up by even a small force. Jeans believed that the gaseous trail was broken up by the sun's gravitational pull. He thought it then cooled, shrank, and finally formed planets. While the sun's gravitational pull was breaking up the trail, the intruder star was moving out into the vastness of space, an unknown parent of our solar system.

According to this theory, the intruder star carried the gaseous trail a long way out before the sun's gravitational pull finally took complete control of the trail. This caused the orbits of the newly formed planets to have the shape of very flat ellipses—like greatly stretched-out circles.

Today, however, the orbits of the planets are only slightly elliptical. Jeans explained this change in the character of the orbits by saying that in addition to the long trail of material ripped from the sun there must have been other large amounts of solar matter thrown all around the sun, creating a cloud of material through which the planets would have had to plow. Physicists know that when an object has to go through any kind of resisting material, whether it be a cloud of solar matter or a block of wood, the object has to spend energy to get through it. It was supposed by Jeans and the other supporters of this theory that as the newly formed planets passed through the remains of the gaseous material ripped from the sun, their long, egg-shaped orbits slowly changed into the nearly circular orbits that the planets follow today.

Jeans's tidal theory has not found many supporters in recent years because it has not been able to account for the fact that the planets spin or rotate about their own axes in addition to orbiting the sun. The other major objection to this theory is that unless one assumes that the sun was very much larger than it is now, it is impossible to understand how the passing star would have been able to carry the gaseous material ripped from the sun out to the great distances where one now finds the planets. The material would have simply scattered into space long before it could condense into a planet. For example, in the case of the planet Uranus, the intruder star would have had to pull material equivalent to fourteen earths a distance of 1,800 million miles from the sun. This theory has now been almost completely discarded as a possible explanation for the origin of the earth.

A Companion for the Sun

When the tidal theory failed to explain how the planetary material was carried out to great distances and then set into nearly circular orbits, astronomers began to look for other theories of creation. Henry N. Russell, an American astronomer who is well known for his discovery of the relation between a star's apparent color and its brightness, came up with an idea that took away the main objection to the tidal hypothesis. He supposed that our sun at one time was part of a binary-star combination. A *binary star* is really two stars orbiting about a point in space called their common center of gravity.

Russell reasoned that if a third star were to approach rather closely our sun's twin companion, it would raise tides on the twin just as Jeans suggested in his tidal theory. These tides would rip enough material out of the giant twin to form our solar system.

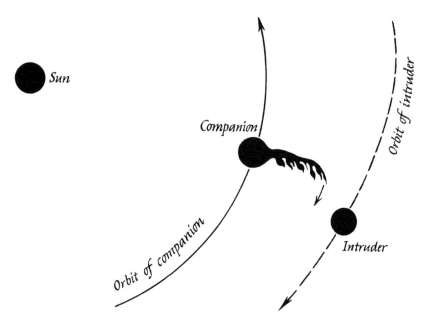

H. N. Russell believed that an intruder star raised huge tides on a companion star to the sun. The planets then formed out of the tidal material.

The suggestion that our sun was part of a binary system is not an unreasonable one. Binary stars are very common in our galaxy. At least one tenth of all stars relatively near us are considered to be part of twin-star systems.

Russell and the other astronomers who supported Russell's idea believed that the orbit of the companion star was about 1,800 million miles from the sun, the same distance away as the present orbit of the planet Uranus. Their calculations showed that if the twin star was the same size as the sun, it would take about fifty years for it to make a trip around the sun. If a third star, the intruder, passed within 3 or 4 million miles of the twin, it would pull a long trail of gaseous material from it. But the intruder would be so far from the sun that it would produce almost no tides there. Additional calculations showed that after their near collision, both the twin and the intruder star might disappear into space. However, some of the material removed from the twin might go into ellipse-shaped orbits around the sun. The planets would then be formed by the same cooling and shrinking process that was described in the tidal theory. When the newly formed planets, not yet solid, came near each other, the tidal forces between them might have produced satellites like our moon.

While this theory does successfully explain certain things about the origin of our solar system, it fails to explain several important points. If the planets were all formed by the intruder at about the same distance from the sun, by what process were the planets placed in their greatly different present-day orbits?

Another difficulty with the theory of a visiting star involves the number of planetary systems that are believed to exist. It is known that distances between stars are very great. Consider a ball that is 30 light-years across with our sun at the center. In that ball there are only about forty star systems. With so few stars in such a large volume of space it would seem that two stars would rarely approach one another. If planets are formed when gases are pulled out from stars during close approaches, then one would not expect to find many planets.

Though astronomers cannot see planets in other solar systems, they have been able, in several cases, to observe the influence that planets have on stars which they can see. Astronomers now estimate that at least one star in a thousand, and perhaps one in a hundred, may be surrounded by a planetary system. In our galaxy alone this would mean that at least 100 million stars have planets traveling with them.

The binary-star hypothesis was designed to show how the planets could attain orbits at great distances from the sun, and it does this very well. However, despite the clever ideas presented in this hypothesis, it still has shortcomings too great for it to be considered a satisfactory explanation of the creation of the planets.

None of the theories presented here is today thought to be a correct explanation of our solar system's origin. They are important nonetheless, because they reawakened the interest of astronomers in the creation of the planets. Now most scientists feel that a satisfactory explanation of the creation of our solar system can come only from a theory that explains not just the origin of the planets but also the origin of the sun. None of these three theories could do that.

THE NEBULAR IDEA OF
CREATION

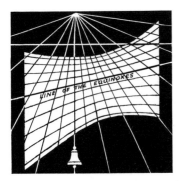

ONE OF THE earliest scientific ideas that was proposed to explain the creation of the sun, the earth, and the other planets is called the nebular theory. It was first suggested by a German philosopher, Immanuel Kant, in 1755. About forty years later, Pierre Simon de Laplace, a French mathematician, changed some of the details in Kant's theory and so today this is sometimes called the Kant-Laplace theory of creation.

Their theory was accepted for almost one hundred years—a long time for a scientific explanation of creation to last. It has recently become popular again, though it has been slightly changed because of our increased knowledge about the abundance of the elements in our universe.

Kant assumed that in the beginning a great cloud of gas spread out into space beyond the orbit of Saturn, then the outermost known planet. This giant gaseous cloud was slowly drawn inward toward its center and then, Kant assumed, it began to rotate automatically. As the gas cloud shrank, the speed of rotation increased. Most of the gas went into the central part of the rotating cloud, became very hot, and began to form the sun. The rest of the gas coalesced into smaller globs to make the planets. These globular masses rotated around the sun and their own axes in the direction of rotation of the original cloud.

Laplace's Theory

Kant's theory was ignored by the scientific community, and when Laplace presented a somewhat similar idea in 1796 he seemed to know nothing about Kant's idea. Laplace's creation hypothesis improved on Kant's in one very important detail. Laplace, who knew a lot about the motion of heavenly bodies, did not assume that the giant cloud would automatically start rotating; he merely assumed that it was already rotating and did not bother to explain how the rotation got started. He stated that at first the gas cloud rotated very slowly and the gravitational pull of the particles making up the cloud caused it to shrink more and more. As it shrank its rotational speed became faster and faster, just as an ice skater turning slowly with his arms extended, suddenly starts spinning very fast when he draws his arms close to his body. Initially, when the gas cloud was large and rotating slowly, it carried the same *angular momentum* as after the cloud had shrunk in size and was turning much faster. The reason for this is that the angular momentum, or tendency of a rotating body to keep on turning, must remain the same.

Laplace had doubts about his own theory and cautioned his readers that it might be incorrect. It had, in fact, a fatal weakness. He knew that the angular momentum is not distributed equally between the sun and the planets. Most of the mass of the solar system is concentrated in the sun, but the planets have 98 percent of the angular momentum of the system, and

An ice skater's tendency to keep on rotating is the same wherever he holds his arms. With his arms extended he rotates slowly, but as he pulls them in, he speeds up in accordance with the law of conservation of angular momentum.

the sun has only the remaining 2 percent. Laplace's theory failed to explain how the sun could lose so little of its mass but nearly all of its angular momentum to the planets. In time, other weaknesses in the theory became evident.

But the nebular idea of the creation of the solar system was not to be dismissed easily. It has been studied and restudied and scientists are still interested in it. Their interest is kept alive by their growing knowledge of nebulae and other areas of science, primarily chemistry.

Von Weizsäcker's Theory

Many years ago when astronomers started to observe nebulae with their telescopes, they saw great black spots in these giant formations of gas. Study of these spots, which are probably enormous globs of dust and gas partly stuck together, show that the globs have at least as much material in them as there is in our sun. The distance between these giant gas collections is about the same as the distance between the sun and nearby stars. These balls of dust, gas, and ice are sometimes called *protostars*, which means stars that are in an early stage of formation.

Recently Carl F. von Weizsäcker, a German astronomer, using his knowledge of protostars and Laplace's theory of a giant nebula, came up with a planetary creation theory that has been well received among scientists. His theory ties in nicely with the big-bang or evolutionary creation theory of the universe because he suggests that the initial tremendous explosion would create giant swirls of matter throughout space.

Von Weizsäcker supposed that the solar system was born from a huge mass of gas and dust that formed a nebula slowly revolving about its own center. Although it sounds impossible, light from nearby stars might have helped gravity to push the slower-moving parts of the cloud toward the center and form the protostar of what is now the sun.

Scientists have found that some things about light can be explained only if light is considered to be made up of tiny packets of energy called *photons*. If a stream of photons (a light beam) is directed onto a body, it can exert a pressure on the body in the same way that a collection of gas molecules can exert a pressure on the walls of a compressed-air tank. The light pressure is very small and can be measured only with very special instruments. The pressure of sunlight, sometimes called the *solar wind*, is usually given as the reason that

A gaseous nebula in the constellation Sagittarius. The small dark areas which can be seen in nebulae like this one may be the beginning stages of the birth of new stars.

a comet's tail always points away from the sun whether or not the comet is going toward or away from the sun.

Von Weizsäcker believes that the faster-rotating parts of

the nebula flattened into a thin disk spread out from the central ball of gas. Once the gases started to move toward the center, the pull of gravity grew stronger, causing the gas and dust ball to collapse into an even smaller volume. When a gas is pushed into a small volume, it gets hot. (This is easily demonstrated by feeling the barrel of a bicycle air pump after a tire has been filled with it.) As the gas cloud continued to collapse, the temperature in the middle of the cloud reached several million degrees, which is hot enough to start the process by which stars burn. Von Weizsäcker believes that it may have been in just this way that our sun as well as billions of other stars came into existence.

So far this theory is not too different from the ideas of Kant and Laplace, but von Weizsäcker made use of the increased knowledge of the elements now found to be most plentiful in the solar system. It had been supposed until a few decades ago that the elements found most abundantly on earth—oxygen, iron, silicon, etc.—are also most abundant on all the other planets in the solar system, the sun itself, and the universe in general. This is now known to be incorrect. The sun and the other stars are 99 percent hydrogen and helium, with all the other elements sharing the remaining 1 percent. Von Weizsäcker and others proposed that the original nebula out of which our sun and planets were formed must have consisted almost completely of a hydrogen-helium mixture containing no more than 1 percent of the heavier elements. Hydrogen and helium are very light gases and they would, in time, drift away from the nebula into space. That would leave behind the molecules and dust of the heavier elements, which would gradually gather into even larger particles. Since the heavier elements are believed to have made up only a tiny fraction of the original nebula, then in order for the nine planets to have been born from the original gaseous disk it must have had a mass at least hundreds of times bigger than the mass of all the planets today.

After the gas ball had flattened into a disk, the general motion of the whole nebula gradually gave way to separate swirls of matter revolving about the new sun in individual orbits. These new swirls of dust, gas, and ice began to stick together to form *protoplanets*, or new planets. Von Weizsäcker believes that smaller swirls around the main swirls then gave rise to moonlike satellites around the protoplanets. A simplified drawing showing the possible directions of the swirls is shown in the diagram. The material in the disk continued to churn about. Every now and then one collection of

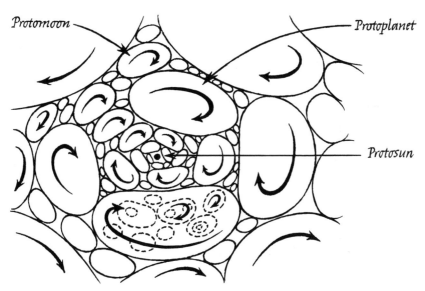

The swirling whirls and eddies that formed in the solar nebula and out of which the planets coalesced according to von Weizsäcker and others.

gas and dust would collide with another, and the gravitational pull would be strong enough to hold both of them together. As this new planet moved around the new sun, it would sweep up additional dust, gas, and ice.

Both protostars and protoplanets were cool in the beginning. Even if the new sun had given off a lot of energy, there was so much dust between it and the new planets that most of the energy would not have reached the planets. At first, the protoplanets were like little suns themselves, mostly hydrogen and helium gas. Then, as the protoplanets grew smaller, the heavier parts sank to the center, leaving ice and sandlike materials near the surface to form a thick blanket around the heavy center. An envelope of light gases covered the surfaces of the new planets. During the millions of years that protoplanets were forming into the planets seen today, the protosun was growing smaller. After 100 million years of compression of the gases that made up the protosun, the temperature was high enough to begin the process in which hydrogen is converted to helium—the fusion process that man has been able to duplicate in hydrogen bombs. This process destroys a small amount of mass but releases a tremendous amount of heat and light.

As the temperature of the sun rose, more and more heat, light, protons, and electrons reached the protoplanets. This solar wind given off by the sun pushed away the light gases of hydrogen and helium from the new planets in the same way that light from nearby stars may have helped push together the cloud that formed the solar system. For a while, the solar system must have looked like a collection of giant comets with their luminous tails stretching far out into space. This stage of development must have lasted until most of the

About 5 billion years ago the material that made up the solar system existed in space as a very thin gas and dust cloud.

After several hundred million years some of the gas and dust coalesced into a ball, still surrounded by a thin gas disk.

With time the ball in the center and the disk became more compact.

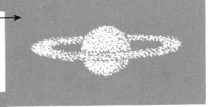

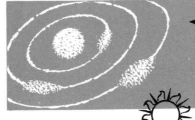

Gravitational attraction between the particles in the central ball became stronger, compressing the parts together enough to start the fusion reaction that produces the heat and light given off by the sun. The material in the disk started to form into protoplanets.

The solar wind from→ the sun blew away the rest of the disk as the protoplanets formed into planets, leaving the solar system much as it is seen today.

hydrogen and helium gases around the inner planets were blown away.

The big advantage of von Weizsäcker's theory is that it fits very well what is known about the solar system today. The swirling eddies of gas around the protosun nucleus provide a good explanation of why the original nebular disk broke up into several planets instead of forming just one. The swirls closest to the sun were kept small because at that close distance the sun's gravitational pull would be so great that it would rob them of their building material. According to von Weizsäcker, an inner band of smaller eddies gave rise to the small planets Mercury, Venus, Earth, and Mars, while farther out, where the sun's gravitational pull is less, an outer band of larger eddies resulted in the giant planets Jupiter, Saturn, Uranus, and Neptune.

Relative size of the planets in comparison with the sun. The distance each planet is from the sun is not shown accurately on this drawing; however, the planets are shown in the order they are from the sun.

At greater distances from the sun the solar wind was weak and thus unable to drive off the hydrogen out of which the planets were born. Jupiter and Saturn are rich in hydrogen today, containing about the same relative amount of hydrogen as the sun. The makeup of the atmospheres of Uranus and Neptune, located farther away from us, has not been determined with certainty, but these planets are believed to be poor in hydrogen. Mercury, the planet closest to the sun, has been exposed to a strong solar wind, leaving it with a rocky surface with little or no gases surrounding it.

At first the protoplanets were cool, and even the protosun was relatively cool. In fact they were so cool that many of the planetesimal lumps were made up of gases that had condensed into liquids (just as steam when cooled will condense into water and then freeze into ice). Particles of dry dirt or dust do not hang together, but when wet they do—as mud. The liquids that condensed out of the gases therefore served as glue, gathering and sticking dust and other small particles together until the lumps became large enough to draw and hold other matter by gravitational pull. Initially the gravitational pull was weak, but it grew stronger as the globs of mud and ice increased in mass. Close to the sun, where the temperature was fairly high, only iron and sandlike materials were able to condense from a gas to a liquid and thus serve as a glue. Farther out, at the present orbit of Mars, water and ammonia condensed and were used in the formation of mud. Beyond the orbit of Mars it was so cold that water and ammonia would freeze to a dry, hard solid and could not make a mud. In the cooler region from Jupiter outward, methane, the major component in natural gas, served as a glue.

The next step in the planet-building process occurred as the lumps of dust, dirt, and some gluelike liquid began to shrink toward a more solid condition. The shrinking and compression started to raise the temperature on the planet. At the higher temperatures gases began to expand and thus be driven away from the planet. That left behind the molecules and dust of the heavier elements and compounds. These gradually gathered into larger particles and into mixed lumps of matter, which formed the planet cores. The heat at the interior was greater in the bigger planets and less in the smaller planets and their satellites. The weaker gravitational pull of the smaller bodies resulted in less compacting and heating and retention of less atmosphere. Small planets like Mercury and Mars became solid before the large amounts of iron and nickel that had been swept up by the protoplanets could sink through to their centers. On larger planets like the earth and Venus, these heavy metals could sink down through the rocks, which were still hot and soft, to form a heavy and hot liquid center. This process is still going on; part of the earth's interior is believed to consist of heavy metals at temperatures high enough to keep them liquid.

One recent idea that has been added to von Weizsäcker's nebular theory helps explain the distribution of angular momentum between the planets and the sun. This theory agrees that our solar system formed from a giant disk of rotating gas, out of which the sun condensed. But it adds that by means of magnetic forces the newly formed sun pushed and pulled different parts of the gaseous disk, out of which the planets were born. A magnetic force can produce the same effect on a body as a gravitational force. The force that a horseshoe magnet exerts on a nearby nail is an example of a magnetic force.

It now takes the sun about 26 days to make a complete rotation, but it is believed that when the sun was new it turned much faster. Because it was turning so fast and had so much mass, it had most of the angular momentum, or tendency to keep on rotating, of the solar system, while the gaseous disk out of which the planets were formed had very little. Using its magnetic forces, the sun was able to push and pull the whirling eddies and swirls in the gaseous disk. The pushing and pulling of the gas cloud took angular momentum from the hub of the nebula (the sun), thus slowing it down. It delivered this momentum to the rim of the nebula (the gaseous disk) by means of its magnetic forces, thus speeding it up. In this way angular momentum was transferred from the protosun to the protoplanets. This idea has been helped along by astronomers' discovering that not only the sun but all the observable stars seem to be able to exert magnetic forces.

If the nebular theory or one similar to it is correct, and many scientists today think it is, then planets can be produced in the normal condensing of a star out of nebular matter, without any help from another star. That is, no passing star is needed to raise tides, encourage prominences, or engage in collisions to create a planetary system. If planets are born out of the gaseous material from which stars evolve, then the universe should be full of planet families, and among them should be many planets with conditions suitable to create and sustain life. Some scientists speculate that a few have beings as intelligent as man, while some planets may have beings considerably more intelligent than earth people.

A FINAL WORD

 MANY PEOPLE BELIEVE the world came to be without whirling nebulae, diving ducks, gigantic companion stars, or giant cows. Some of these people believe that the creation of the world was an event both so beautiful and so amazing that only God could have caused such a thing to happen. This creation story is told in the Bible.

Modern scholars who study the Bible now recognize that there are two accounts of creation given in Genesis. The first story is said to have been compiled by a group of men called the Priestly school about twenty-five hundred years ago. This story was probably based on a Babylonian creation story. The origins of the Babylonian story go back another thousand years, and some scholars believe it might be even older than that. That the Priestly school had poets in it cannot be denied since this story of creation is as beautiful and simply told as any we have met.

> In the beginning God created the heaven and the earth.
>
> And the earth was without form, and void; and the darkness was upon the face of the deep. And the Spirit of God moved upon the face of the waters.
>
> And God said, Let there be light: and there was light.
>
> And God saw the light, that it was good: and God divided the light from the darkness.
>
> And God called the light Day, and the darkness he

called Night. And the evening and the morning were
the first day.

On the second day God turned his attention to both the
waters and the heavens:

> And God made the firmament, and divided the wa-
> ters which were under the firmament from the waters
> which were above the firmament: and it was so.

And on the third day,

> . . . God said, Let the waters under the heaven be
> gathered together unto one place, and let the dry land
> appear: and it was so.

He then made the plants and trees of the earth. God in the
next few days created the seasons, the sun, the moon, the
stars, the animals, and the birds. Then He created man in His
own image, finishing His efforts on the sixth day.

> And God saw everything that he had made, and, be-
> hold, it was very good . . . .
> And on the seventh day God ended his work which
> he had made; and he rested on the seventh day from all
> his work which he had made.

The second story of creation that is told in Genesis is also
believed to have come, at least in part, from Babylonia. According to this tale, the earth was a barren wasteland already
in existence and on it the Lord planted a beautiful garden "to
the East of Eden." Man was created from the dust of the
ground and the Lord breathed into his nostrils the breath of
life. Man went to live in the garden, and there he was soon
joined by all the animals of the world, as well as by a wife.
This is the familiar story about Adam and Eve in the Garden
of Eden.

And so this is how it was in the beginning according to the Bible of the Jews and Christians. They have passed these stories down to us for over two thousand years, practically unchanged.

There are stories of creation thousands of years old and stories of creation a few years old. Only one theory of creation can be scientifically correct, and we may not yet know what it is. Was it the sun or some other unknown star that was the true parent of our solar system? At present there is only one thing scientists can agree on when it comes to creation: No one, so far, has come up with a creation theory that all scientists can conclude is correct.

So we cannot give a single, absolute answer to the important question, "How did our world come to be?" Will we always be puzzled about our beginnings? When we consider how much scientists do discover each year, it seems reasonable to suppose that we will get closer to the true story of creation as time goes by.

The information that satellites and space rockets send back to us each year adds to the storehouse of knowledge about our solar system. That information along with what we have learned already with our telescopes and radio telescopes allows scientists to replace some of the guesses in their theories with facts. While it is true that we have discarded the Coyote-man of the Crow Indians and the golden egg of the Hindus, there is still no creation story built completely on facts. But that should not discourage us. Man has been curious about the birth of the world for a long time. For 5,000 years people have tried to understand creation. But 5,000 years are like

The earth from 22,300 miles in space as
photographed from NASA's ATS-III satellite.

a fleeting instant for the 5,000,000,000-year-old planet on
which we live.

65

GLOSSARY

angular momentum—a measure of a rotating body's tendency to keep on rotating.

asteroid—one of a number of small planets nearly all of whose orbits lie between those of Mars and Jupiter.

astronomy—the study of the motion, composition, and position of the stars and other heavenly bodies in the universe.

atoms—tiny bits of matter from which all materials are made. Atoms consist of a central core, or nucleus, of protons and neutrons and an outer shell of electrons.

axis—a line around which a turning body rotates. For example, a wheel turns about its axle, which is its axis.

binary-star system—two stars, relatively close together, rotating about a point in space called their common center of gravity.

binding force—the force that holds the protons in a nucleus together. At very short distances it is strong enough to overcome the force of repulsion that always exists between like electric charges.

coalesce—the growing or coming together of many parts into one.

comet—a collection of meteorlike fragments that form a head with a trail of very fine gases and dust that can stretch for millions of miles. Most comets are thought to be in orbit about the sun.

constellation—any group of stars imagined to represent the outline of a being or thing. Many constellations were named long ago.

deuteron—the double-weight hydrogen atom nucleus containing one proton and one neutron. This nucleus plus an orbiting electron make up the deuterium atom.

electron—a very small particle found in atoms. It carries a negative electric charge. When electricity flows in a wire, it is thought to be the movement of electrons.

67

element—a collection of a particular kind of atom, each of which has the same number of protons in its nucleus. Elements cannot be separated into simpler substances by ordinary chemical means.

ellipse—the shape of a flattened circle produced by keeping constant the sum of the distances between two points. The orbits that the planets follow are ellipse-shaped.

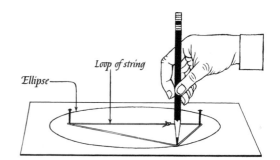

An ellipse-shaped fig-ure may be drawn us-ing two tacks, a loop of string, and a pencil as shown.

fusion—the process that is believed to take place in stars and has now been copied by man in the hydrogen bomb in which four hydro-gen atoms are joined together to make one helium atom. This process releases a tremendous amount of energy as heat and light.

galaxy—a very large system of stars, nebulae, and other heavenly bodies. Our solar system is a part of the galaxy called the Milky Way.

gravity—the pull or force of attraction that exists between all bodies.

helium—next to hydrogen the most abundant atom in the universe. The helium atom consists of two protons and two neutrons in the nucleus orbited by two electrons. After hydrogen, helium is the lightest gas found in nature.

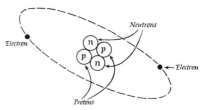

The makeup of an atom of helium.

hydrogen—the simplest, lightest, and most abundant atom in the universe. It consists of one proton and one orbiting electron.

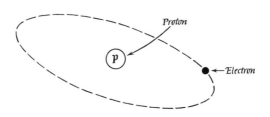

The makeup of a hydrogen atom.

hypothesis—an unproved explanation taken from observed facts and used as a basis for further investigation.

light-year—the distance traveled by light in one year going 186,000 miles per second. It is equivalent to a distance of 5,870 billion miles.

mass—the quantity of matter in a body as measured by its tendency to resist motion. It takes a bigger push to get a larger mass up to a certain speed in a given time interval than it does a smaller mass.

meteor—small stonelike bodies that enter the earth's atmosphere at great speed. The air friction heats them up to such high temperatures that they generally produce a visible streak of light across the sky.

Milky Way—one of the billions of galaxies in the universe. It consists of the sun, all the other stars that can be seen with the naked eye, plus millions of other nearby stars. Sometimes astronomers call it "the Galaxy" because for man it is indeed the most important galaxy in the universe.

myth—an imaginary story usually explaining some phenomenon of nature. It frequently involves heroes, gods, or other beings with supernatural abilities.

nebula—a cloudlike body found in our galaxy and others consisting mostly of hydrogen but also of other light gases and dust. A nebula frequently gives off a faint glow or shines by the reflected light from nearby stars, which allows it to be seen with sensitive telescopes. More than one nebula are called *nebulae*.

neutron—a very small particle found in atoms. It has no electric charge.

nucleus—the heart of an atom, consisting of neutrons and positively charged protons. The nucleus in an atom is normally surrounded by a swarm of negatively charged electrons.

observable universe—that portion of the universe moving away from our solar system with a speed slower than the speed of light, thus making it visible from the earth, at least in theory. Galaxies closer to the earth than about 13 billion light-years are within the observable universe.

orbit—the path in space along which a heavenly body or a man-made satellite moves.

photon—the energy-carrying packet of which light is sometimes thought to be composed.

physicist—one who studies the laws governing matter and energy.

planet—bodies which orbit a star and are incapable of producing any light of their own. They can be seen only by light from the star they orbit that is reflected off their surface.

prominence—a giant eruption of gases on the surface of a star.

proton—a very small particle found in atoms. It carries a positive electric charge.

protoplanet—a planet in an early stage of formation.

protostar—a star in an early stage of formation.

radioactivity—a change that occurs in certain unstable atoms as they continuously give off nuclear particles. A radioactive atom will continue to change until it has reached a stable condition.

rotate—to turn about an axis. A wheel rotates about its axle.

scientific method—a plan of study used to learn about nature by the careful testing of hypotheses with observations. Theories about nature found in this way are frequently discarded when new evidence shows them to be wrong.

solar system—the sun and all the heavenly bodies (planets, moons, asteroids, and comets) that revolve about the sun.

solar wind—the stream of photons, electrons, and protons that is thrown from the sun in all directions.

supernova—a star whose brightness increases so rapidly and dramatically that it appears to be exploding.

universe—the collection of everything there is; it includes all galaxies, nebulae, and other heavenly bodies.

ylem—the very hot primordial mixture of neutrons, protons, and electrons from which, Gamow believed, the universe was born.

INDEX

About the Author

When his oldest son, Joshua, asked how the world began, Stanley W. Angrist realized he didn't know the answer. He began to do research on the question, and soon became fascinated by the numerous myths and scientific theories that there are on the subject. The result of his reading and study is *How Our World Came to Be*, Dr. Angrist's first book for young people.

An Associate Professor of Mechanical Engineering at the Carnegie-Mellon University, Dr. Angrist lives with his wife and two sons in Pittsburgh, Pennsylvania.

About the Illustrator

Enrico Arno has had a distinguished career as a children's book illustrator. He was born in Mannheim, Germany, and educated in Berlin. He emigrated to Italy in 1940, working for Mondrian in Milan and later for a publisher in Rome. Mr. Arno came to the United States in 1947. He and his wife live in Sea Cliff, New York.